NATIONAL GEOGRAPHIC

This Food Grows Here

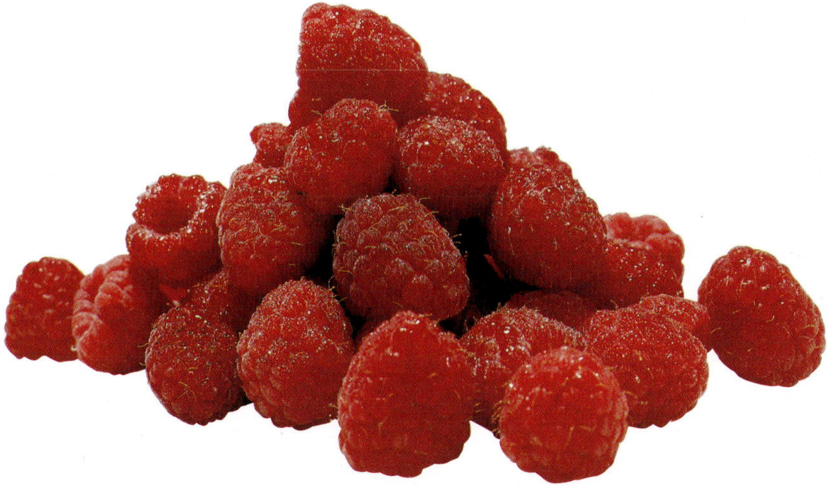

Zoe Sharp

This food grows here.

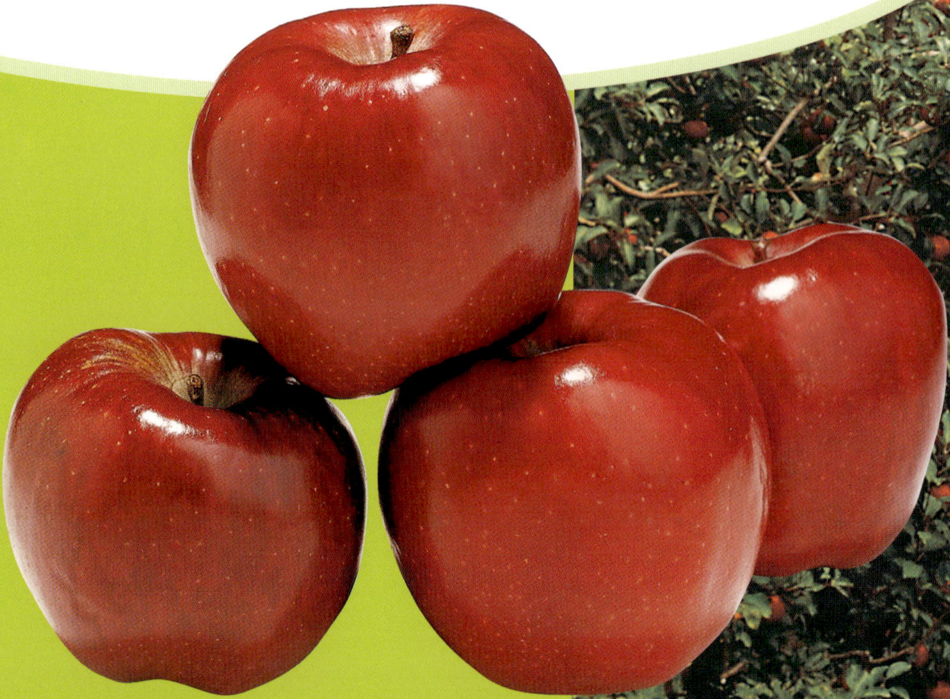

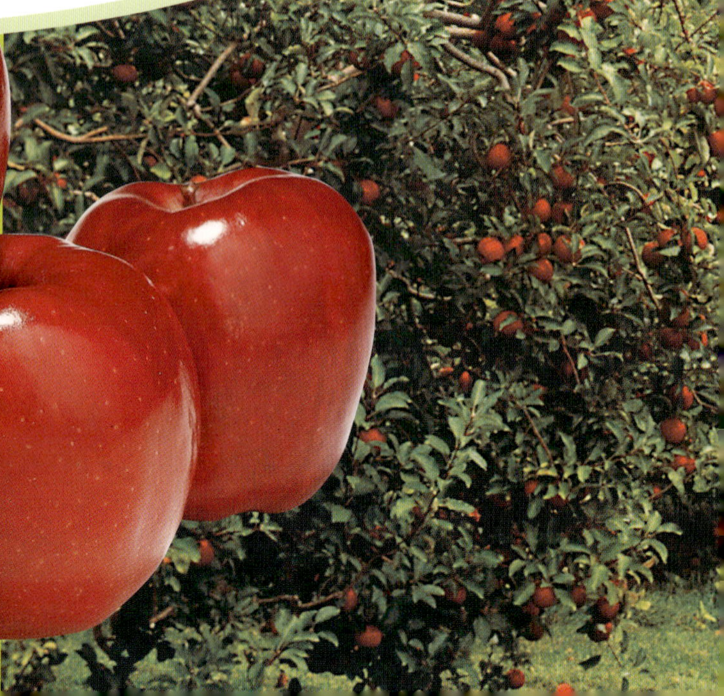

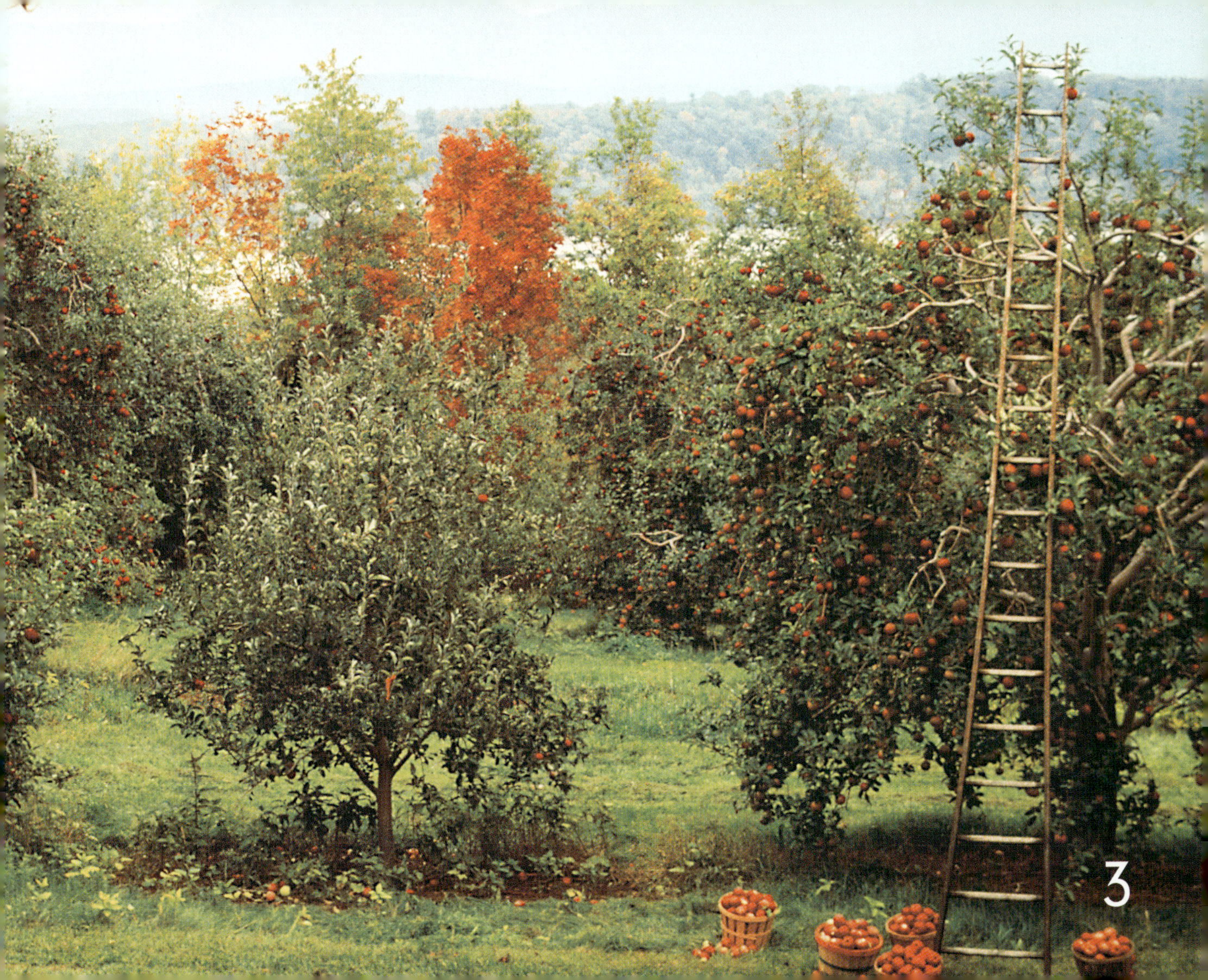

This food grows here.

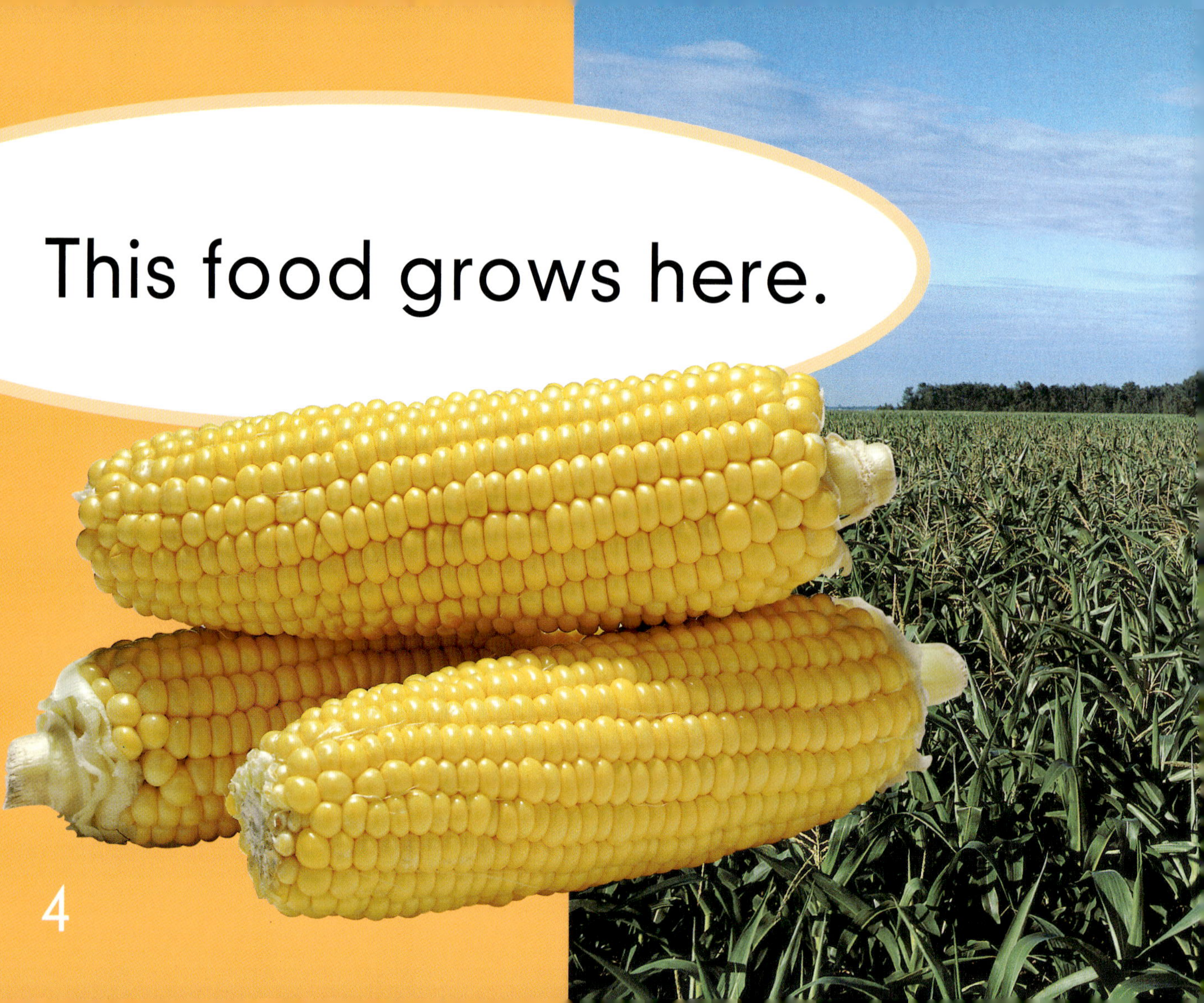

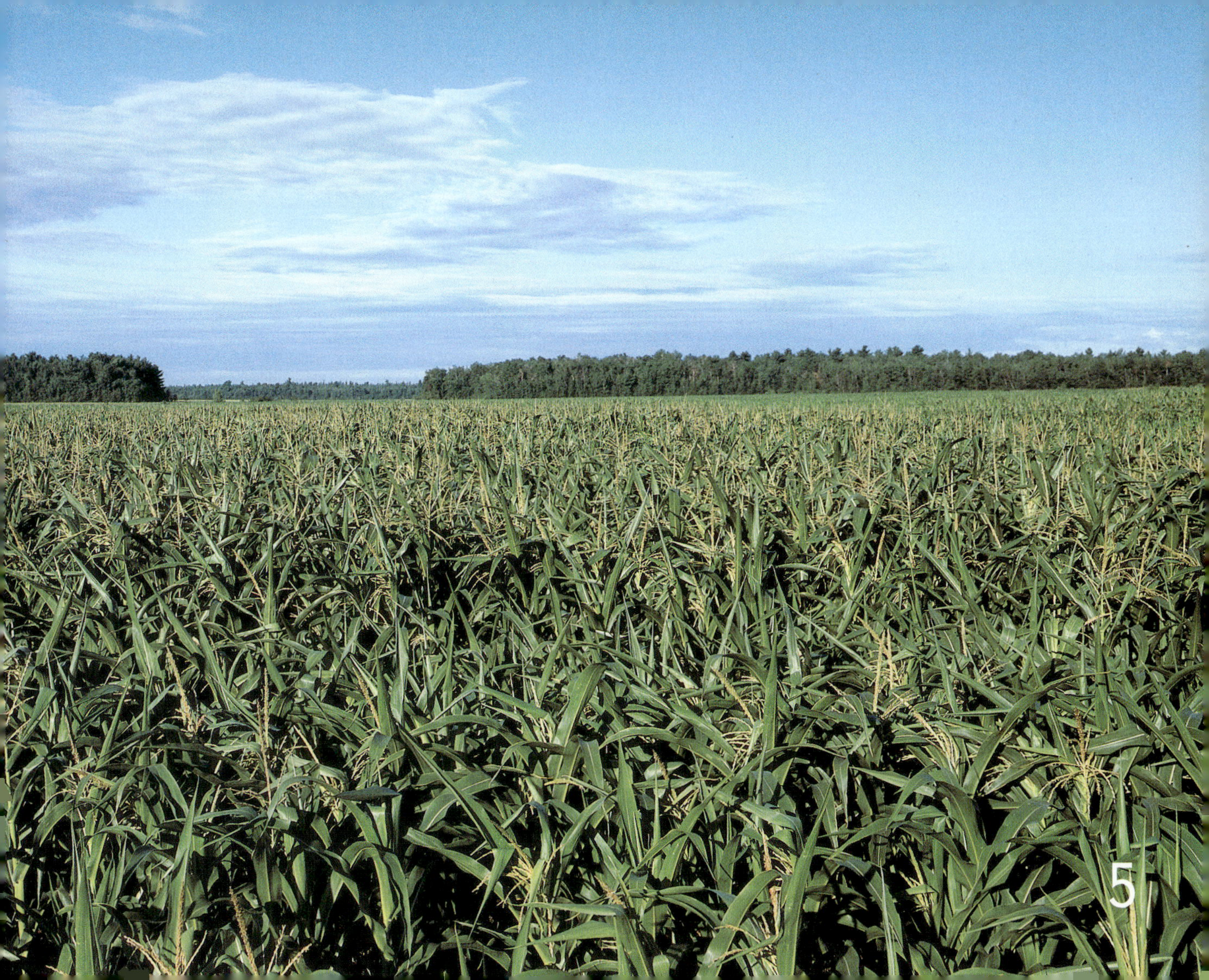

This food grows here.

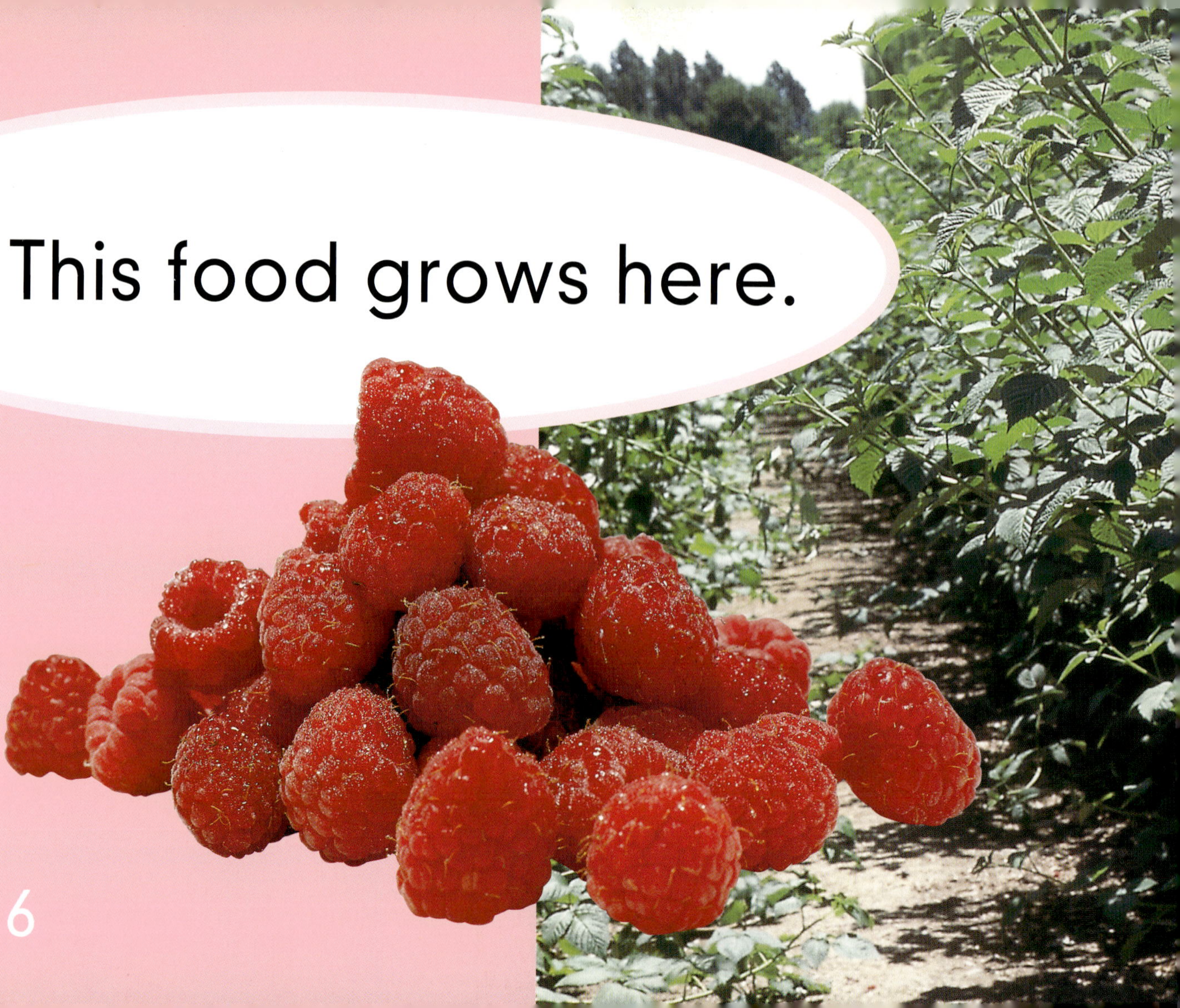

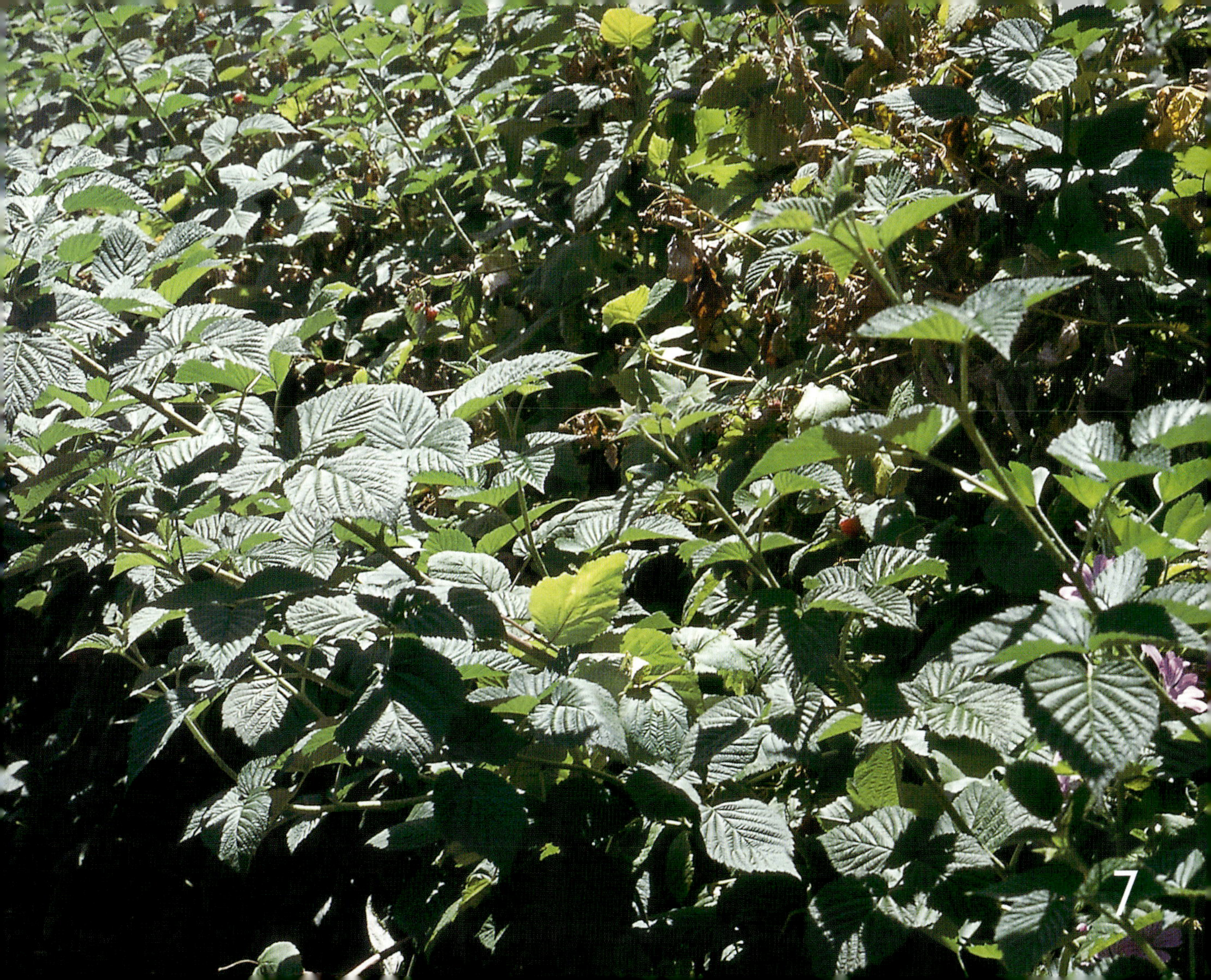

This food grows here.

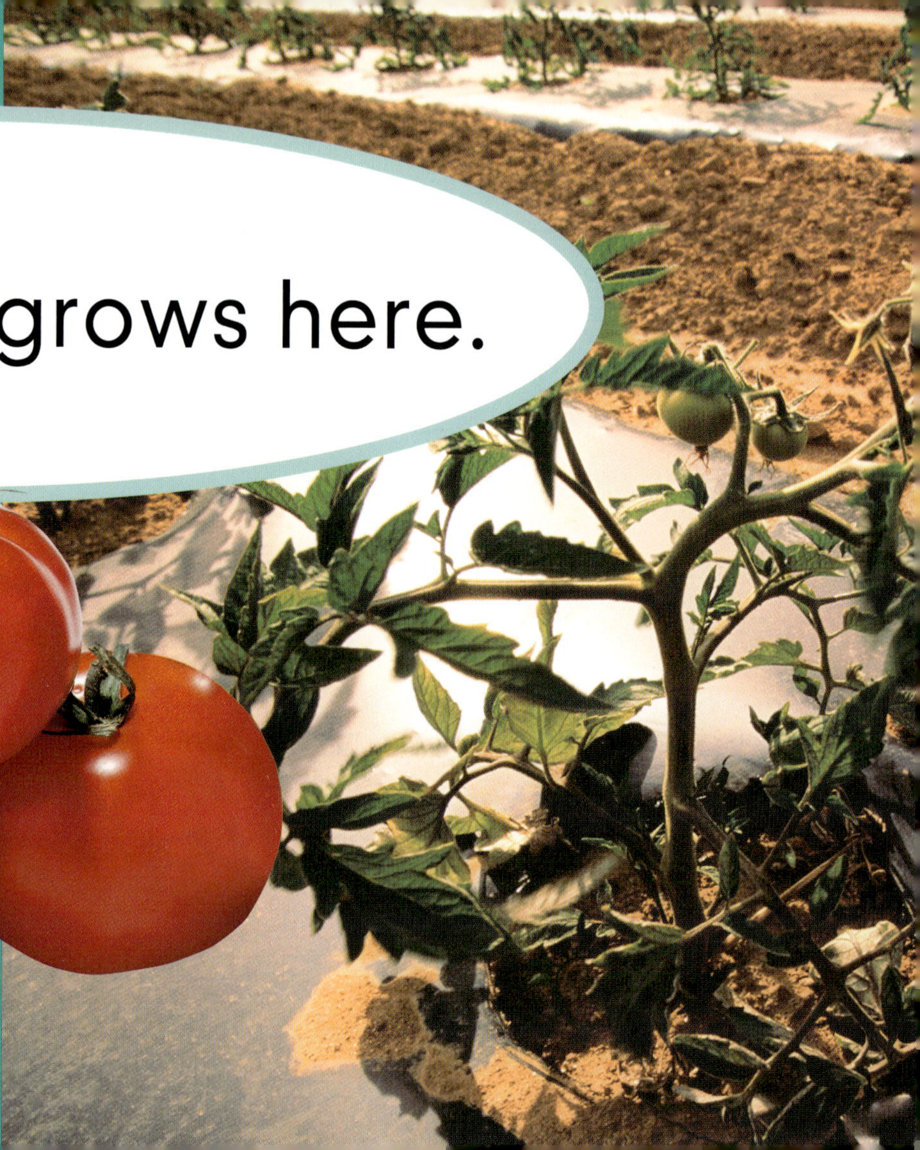

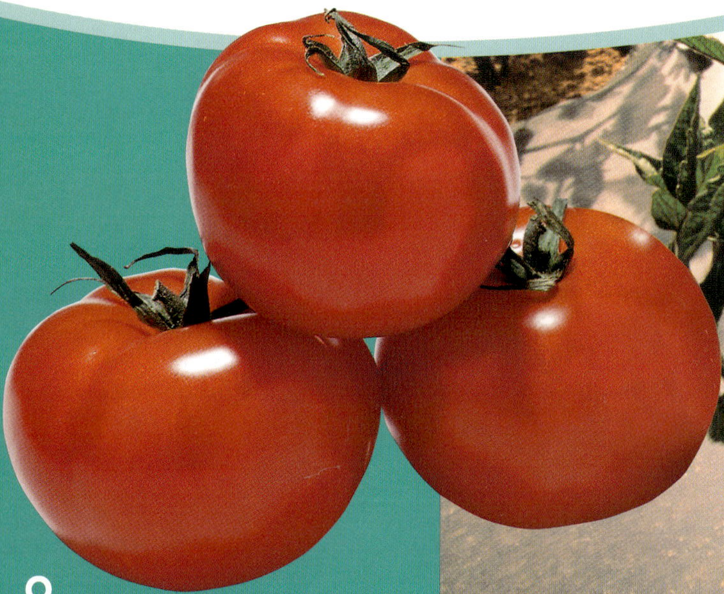